1

TURNING FAITH
INTO POWER

Other Books by S. Richard Nelson

Gaining Power through Prayer

The Added Power of Obedience

The Healing Power of Forgiveness

The Mighty Power of the Word

The Gift and Power of the Holy Spirit

Love: The Only True Power

Sustainable Spirituality

The Faith Factor

This Is Life Eternal

5-star reviews are a blessing to Christian authors. If you find this book inspirational, educational or simply enjoyable, please post an honest review.

The Powerful Christian Series - Book I

TURNING FAITH INTO POWER

By S. Richard Nelson

First Edition published 2012
Second Printing 2013
Third Printing 2015
Fourth Printing June 2019

ISBN-13: 978-0-9852470-0-3
ISBN-10: 0985247002
BISAC: Religion / Christian Life / Spiritual Growth

Broken Hill Publications
Glenwood Springs, CO 81601

Artistic Design by Connie & Stephen Gorton
Edited by Lauren Conley

"From this broken hill,
All your praises they shall ring."

L. Cohen – If It Be Your Will

www.srnelson.com

"For God did not give us a Spirit of fear but of power and love and self-control."

2 Timothy 1:7 (NET)

Table of Contents

A Principle of Power and Action 13

The Center of Our Faith 23

Lord, Increase Our Faith 31

Faith in Yourself 39

Be Not Faithless 47

Faith – The Force of Life 57

About the Author 69

Other Books by Rich Nelson 71

Excerpt: 77

"Faith is much more than merely a manifestation of our belief. Faith is a real power."

Rich Nelson

Chapter 1

A Principle of Power and Action

The Savior says in Matthew 17:20, "For most assuredly I tell you, if you have faith as a grain of mustard seed, you will tell this mountain, 'Move from here to there,' and it will move; and nothing will be impossible to you."

As believing Christians there is a substantial, higher power available to us. It is the power of faith. It is the same power by which God created the worlds. Faith is a principle of action and of power, and by it the faithful Christian can influence any number of circumstances when the occasion warrants. Through the bounteous mercy and love of Jesus Christ we receive His grace - a divine means of strength. The power available to us through Jesus Christ is very real.

We are not alone on this earth, and the purpose God has for us is not to fail but to succeed and ultimately to return to God. The purpose for our earthly existence is to give us experience. Sometimes that experience is pleasant and joyful. Other times it is disheartening and unsatisfying. But in every situation, at every age, and whatever our experience, we have the promise of Jesus Christ, "I am with you always, even to the end of the age." (Matthew 28:20). Life Wi-Fi, faith is an invisible power that keeps us connect to what we need. We need not face each day, each trial, and each opportunity alone.

There are two classifications of faith. The first is faith as certainty. Faith as certainty is the intellectual side of faith. It is faith born from experience; it gives us confidence that a new day will dawn, that spring will follow winter, that growth will occur. It is faith that tells us with surety what is bound to transpire.

The second classification is faith as conviction. Faith as conviction is the emotional side of faith. It is an intentional submission and complete confidence in the power of faith. This is faith that instigates events. It is faith fortified and unbending.

It propels change. It is faith that motivates individuals and societies. It is an awe-inspiring, unequalled power as existent and as imperceptible as electricity.

Both types of faith are necessary.

Together, they create an attitude of conviction in the truthfulness and trustworthiness of something that cannot be plainly evidenced. One of the great definitions of faith is in the Epistle to the Hebrews: "Now faith is assurance of things hoped for, proof of things not seen." (Hebrews 11:1). In this epistle, faith is regarded as the conviction of an unseen God that is even more enduring than the things we see and touch.

Faith is not the same as knowledge; faith must center on something that is not known. It must go beyond established evidence, it must venture into the unknown, and it must traverse the edge of light and step into the darkness. If we demand to know everything, if we require that everything be explained, if we insist that everything has to be quantified, then we have no need for faith.

The expression "seeing is believing" promotes skepticism and doubt. We foster the mindset of "show me first, and then I will believe." We demand proof and substantiation first and make it difficult to accept things on faith. But in the spiritual world it works the other way around and we discover that "believing is seeing!" Spiritual belief precedes spiritual knowledge. When we believe in things that are not seen but are true, then we have faith.

Faith, then, is the assurance we have that things exist that are not seen. It is also the principle of action in all intelligent beings. If we stop and think, we realize that it is faith, and faith only, that is the rousing force of all action in us. Without faith we would remain in a state of inactivity, and all our efforts, both physical and mental, would stop.

Consider and ask yourself this: from your earliest recollection, what motivated you to action? What gave you energy and activity in all of your pursuits? It was the hope you had in the existence of unseen things that motivated you to act in order to obtain those things! We are dependent on our faith for all our knowledge, insight, and intellect. We would never have sought wisdom and intelligence unless we believed that we could acquire them.

What farmer would plant, if he didn't believe he would also reap? Who would have ever asked unless she believed that she would receive? Would you have ever looked for something you lost unless you believed that it could be found? In other words, is there anything that you would have set out to accomplish, either physically or mentally, if you had not previously believed you could achieve it? All of our efforts are dependent on our faith!

Just as faith is the motivating basis of action in our worldly concerns, it is also the cause of action in spiritual matters. Jesus said, "He who believes...will be saved." (Mark 16:16). We receive all of our earthly blessings by faith and likewise we receive all our spiritual blessings by faith.

But faith is not just a principle of action. It is also a principle of power. Paul wrote to the Hebrews, "By faith, we understand that the universe has been framed by the word of God, so that what is seen has not been made out of things which are visible." (Hebrews 11:3). The principle of power that is in God, by which the worlds were made, is faith. It is through this power in God that all things are. All things in heaven, on earth, or under the earth, exist by reason of faith as it exists in HIM! Without faith the world would never have been created; men and women would never have been formed of its dust.

If God formed the earth by faith, then faith is a principle of power. If faith is a power that God uses, then faith must be a principle of power in us as well!

Faith is much more than merely a manifestation of our belief. Faith is a real power. The Holy Scriptures witness the fact that faith is power.

From the eleventh chapter of Hebrews we learn that by faith Abel offered unto God a more excellent sacrifice than Cain. By faith Noah, being warned of God of things not yet seen, moved with godly fear, prepared an ark for the saving of his house. By faith Abraham, when he was called to go to a place which he was to receive for an inheritance, obeyed.... By faith he lived in the land of promise. Through faith Sara received power to conceive, and she bore a child when she was past age. By faith Abraham...offered up Isaac...to whom it was said, in Isaac will your seed be called; accounting that God is able to raise him up. By faith Isaac blessed Jacob and Esau, even concerning things to come.

By faith Moses, when he was born, was hid three months and when he had grown up, refused to be called the son of Pharaoh's daughter; choosing rather to suffer affliction with the people of God, than to enjoy the pleasures of sin;...accounting the reproach of Christ greater riches than the treasures in Egypt. By faith the Israelites passed through the Red sea as by dry land. By faith the walls of Jericho fell down.

The Apostle Paul explains that time would fail him to tell of Gedeon, and of Barak, and of Samson, and of Jephthae; of David also, and Samuel, and of the prophets: who through faith subdued kingdoms, worked out righteousness, obtained promises, stopped the mouths of lions, quenched the power of fire, escaped the edge of the sword, from weakness were made strong, grew valiant in war, turned to fight the armies of aliens. Women received their dead raised to life again.

Also, Joshua, in the sight of all Israel, ordered the sun and moon to stand still, and it was done. (Josh. 10:12-13.)

The Bible teaches us that all things are done by faith. It was by faith that the worlds were framed. God spoke and worlds were formed by the power of faith in Him. The Bible also teaches that this same power of faith is available to human beings. Men spoke by faith in the name of God, and mountains moved, prisons crumbled, lions' mouths were shut, human emotion lost its hostility, fire its fierceness, armies their strength, weapons their fear; even the sun stood motionless, the moon obeyed, and death lost its power; all this by the unspeakable power of faith.

Faith is the prevailing principle of power. In fact, without faith there is no power! Faith is not merely a great motivator. It is an actual power. Faith in the Lord Jesus Christ is an eternal, endless power as great as any power in the whole universe.

"Faith is not the belief that God will do what you want. It is the belief that God will do what is right."

Max Lucado

Chapter 2

The Center of Our Faith

When we reflect on our individual lives on earth, and the variety of viewpoints and values which attempt to explain our existence, is there any spirit we would rather have at the center of our lives than that of Jesus Christ?

The central precept of any Christian is faith in the Lord Jesus Christ. Faith in Him is basic to peace of mind in this life and hopefulness in the world to come. When we center our confidence, hope, and trust in this one solitary figure, with untiring effort, we can become stronger than anything that can happen to us. The essential aspect of our faith centers in the all-wise, all-powerful, and all-benevolent Redeemer and Savior. Only Jesus Christ is uniquely qualified to provide hope, confidence, and strength to subdue the world and rise above social weakness.

This is the reason we center our faith and trust in Him and attempt to live by His example and teachings. Jesus Christ is the Lord God Omnipotent. He was selected before He was born. He is the foundation of life and light to all things. His word is the edict by which all things are directed. Everything formed by Him is subject to His immeasurable power.

Jesus Christ is the Son of God. He came to earth through a royal birthright. Merged in His character were the human features of His mother Mary and the divine qualities and power of His Eternal Father. This unique heritage gave Him the title of the Only Begotten Son of God. As the Son of God, He received powers and intellect that no mere mortal has ever had. He was literally Immanuel, or "God with us".

Jesus was exposed to all the problems and troubles of humanity yet was perfectly obedient to all the laws of God. He submitted to the will of the Father and grew from grace to grace.

By understanding who Jesus is, we can better comprehend how He had power to heal the sick, cure diseases, raise the dead, and command the elements.

He is the Savior and Redeemer of all mankind and He shouldered the burden of our sins. He was lifted up on the cross. Only He had the power to redeem us from our lost and fallen condition. Only He could voluntarily sacrifice his life to provide us a universal resurrection. Only Jesus Christ was able and willing to accomplish such a redeeming act of love.

We may not understand how He overcame death and sin, but we can appreciate why. He was persuaded by His unselfish, immeasurable love for us. He suffered the pain of sin in Gethsemane. He succumbed to humiliation and insults without complaint or retaliation. He bore the brutal shame of the cross and freely gave Himself up to die. As He stated, "No one takes [my life] from me, but I lay it down by myself. I have power to lay it down, and I have power to take it again." (John 10:18-Italics added).

And so we ask ourselves, "Is all of this true? Did Jesus give His life for us? Was He resurrected from the grave giving us life eternal? What proof is there of this?" There will always be those who doubt. But their questions can be resolved.

Resolution is found through faith. It is found through definite and explicit faith in Christ. When the desire to know that Jesus Christ is the Son of God and gave His life to accomplish the resurrection so that we can live again becomes powerful enough, then we will be motivated to accept the truth.

And the truth is there is no solid, physical evidence that God exists or that Jesus is His divine son. But truth is not necessarily found in factual evidence. The lack of proof in the existence of God does not prove that He does not exist. Lacking the positive proof required by the scientific world, we could easily introduce circumstantial evidence. The wonders of creation and of nature, the exactness of the edicts of physical science, the marvels of the human body and thousands of other phenomena, all attest that there must be a divine Designer who directs the cosmos.

Faith bridges the gap in the absence of concrete corroboration.

What would become of faith if there were irrefutable evidence that God exists? If everything could be verified by effusive evidence there would be no need for faith. It would be eradicated because faith is "the substance of things hoped for, the evidence of things not seen." (Hebrews 11:1 KJV). Faith is evidence! It is the assertion of facts that are otherwise not evident and cannot be proven. Faith in

God and Jesus Christ leads us to the knowledge of their existence and divine nature.

Faith in Jesus Christ is more than simply a pronouncement of belief. Faith in Him entails absolute dependence on Him. He has unbounded power and love. There is no earthly dilemma He cannot solve. He suffered all things and knows how to help us overcome our day-to-day conundrums. Faith means trusting in His wisdom when we are confused and uncertain.

Jesus Christ is the resurrection and the life. (John 11:25). The power to regain His own life was possible because He is the Son of God. He had the power to overcome death. Consequently, we will be resurrected as well. "Because I live, you will live also." (John 14:19).

Jesus was "in all points tempted like we are, yet without sin" (Hebrews 4:15); so, He can assist those who are tempted. (Hebrews 2:18). He is the Prince of Peace and can soothe a tormented soul suffering from sorrow or sin. "Peace I leave with you. My peace I give to you.... Don't let your heart be troubled, neither let it be fearful." (John 14:27).

If we are weak or lacking, He will strengthen and compensate. He can empathize with every failure, inadequacy, insufficiency, or depravity.

There is no hurt His love cannot heal. "Come to me, all you who labor and are heavily burdened, and I will give you rest." (Matthew 11:28).

He is our Savior and Redeemer, perfect in His love for us. As Christians, we demonstrate faith in Him by following His word.

"Faith is like a muscle; the more you exercise it, the stronger it becomes."

Chapter 3

Lord, Increase Our Faith

In Luke 17, Jesus addressed His disciples and cautioned them to be diligent. The apostles, realizing what was required of them, pleaded to the Lord, "Increase our faith." They were shown by the analogy of the mustard seed that, "If you had faith as a grain of mustard seed, you would tell this sycamore tree, 'Be uprooted, and be planted in the sea; and it would obey you." (Luke 17:5, 6). If we act on even the smallest amount of faith, it will allow God to increase our faith in Him.

Our faith is defined by obedience and constant devotion as emphasized in the Parable of the Unprofitable Servant.

"But who is there of you, having a servant plowing or keeping sheep, that will say, when he comes in from the field, 'Come immediately and sit down at the table.' and will not rather tell him, 'Prepare my supper, clothe yourself properly, and serve me, while I eat and drink. Afterward you will eat and drink'? ...Even so you also, when you have done all the things that are commanded you, say, 'We are unworthy servants. We have done our duty.'" (Luke 17:7-10.)

As servants, we might feel that after a hard day's work we are entitled to a little rest and relaxation. But remember that the Master has a right to the servant's time and devotion. The apostles of Jesus Christ had committed themselves entirely to the Master's service. They could not falter nor object no matter what effort or sacrifice was required of them. And though it seems exacting, the best they could do would be no more than their obligation.

Faith is better measured in terms of quality than of quantity.

In proper perspective, the pursuit of faith is our principal project. We reap the ultimate blessings through faith. Increasing faith involves establishing a beginning point, a place to start, a place where the power of faith first finds a home in our human hearts. Faith is found in varying levels and amounts.

One person may have the power and faith to do one thing while another has the power and faith to do something greater.

Faith is like a muscle; the more you exercise it, the stronger it becomes. In order to increase our faith, we must engage in events that cause us to stretch, and we must pray that we will be able to accomplish God's will in these tasks we have set for ourselves. Those are the times when we grow. Those are the times when we increase our faith. If we only try to do what we know we are capable of doing, we are not going to grow much. We must look beyond where we are and what we are capable of. Then our faith will increase.

One step we can take to increase our faith is to listen to the Word of God.

Paul asks: "How then will they call on him in whom they have not believed?"

Can we pray to a God we don't believe it?

"How will they believe in him whom they have not heard?"

Can we believe in a God we have never heard of?

"How will they hear without a preacher? And how will they preach, except they are sent? As it is written, 'How beautiful are the feet of those who preach the gospel of peace. Who bring glad tidings of good things!'...So faith comes by hearing, and hearing by the word of God." (Romans 10:14-17).

A second step to increase our faith is reading the word of God. The Bible brings us hope that could only come from God.

In problematic situations, knowing how God helped other believers in the scriptures can provide great hope and faith that He will help us also.

Another step toward increasing our faith is to understand that our faith will grow contingent on our personal righteousness. The apostle John wrote of the influential correlation between worthiness and faith.

"Let's not love in word only, neither with the tongue only, but in deed and truth. And by this we know that we are of the truth, and persuade our hearts before him, because if our heart condemns us, God is greater than our heart, and knows all things. Beloved, if our hearts don't condemn us, we have boldness toward God. And whatever we ask, we receive from him, because we keep his commandments, and do the things that are pleasing in his sight." (1 John 3:18-22 Italics added).

If we are trying to be sinless, (not perfect, but at least trying to live by what we know is right,) then we have the promise that what we ask for, the Lord will allow. But when "our hearts condemn us" it becomes very difficult to find the courage to ask God for approval and we won't receive any increase in our faith.

A key element to increasing our faith is to base our actions in our understanding. What do I mean by this? We need to act according to our current awareness and interpretation of God's word.

If we gain a deeper comprehension of a Bible principle and live by that greater awareness, God will bless us with even more light. If we con-template the core beliefs that we already know and then live up to those beliefs, we can expect the Lord to afford us even greater faith.

Faith and hope are profoundly interconnected, and we can increase our faith if we increase our ability to hope. When we apply our faith, we enlarge our hope. With expanded hope in a good cause we exhibit greater faith in its completion. The two go hand-in-hand.

"For we were saved in hope, but hope that is seen is not hope: for who hopes for that which he sees? But if we hope for that which we don't see, then we wait for it with patience." (Romans 8:24-25).

If something already exists, we do not need to hope for it. But Christians have spiritual perceptions that the world cannot see. We perceive spiritually in our hearts and minds all of God's promises and wait patiently for them. This is the hope we have that increases our faith.

Though difficult to accept at times, hindrances, hardships, and misfortunes significantly increase our faith.

It's easy to make a covenant with God but making the covenant is only the beginning. We must also keep the covenant at all cost. God is surely going to test us to see if we will keep the promises we make with Him.

Look closely at your life. What are the sacrifices God wants you to make for Him? Typically, He wants us to sacrifice our sins. And when we sacrifice what the Lord calls for, we see our faith increase.

Our faith can escalate. It can intensify like a shining light. When our deepest doubts become dark and dense, the most penetrating and persistent faith will send a stream of light right through them.

"… but the Lord stood with me and strengthened me."

2 Timothy 4:17

Chapter 4

Faith in Yourself

Most of us suffer from the terrible weakness of lacking faith in ourselves. We often tend to depreciate our enormous worth and value in the sight of God.

How important are you?

Do you treat yourself poorly or like someone of immense value?

Do you see yourself as a son or a daughter of divinity?

Do you have faith in yourself?

From God's perspective, you are extremely valuable. He loves you and desires nothing but joyfulness and pleasure for you. Showing faith in God shows you also have faith in yourself. With

God's help, you can accomplish all things; your potential is unlimited.

As a child of God, you are somebody. Christ will form you, frame you, and amplify you if you walk with Him. How tremendous to recognize your true potential in and through Him! How remarkable to see that in His strength you can do anything! No matter where you find yourself in life, you cannot rationally call yourself a "nobody".

One principal task in life is to lift the "nobody" notion in you to a "somebody" concept who is loved, wanted, and needed. "I'm nobody" is a destructive philosophy and a tool of the deceiver.

"What does it matter? I'm nobody" is heartbreaking to hear.

"I'm no one special. I'm just one of the thousands" is devastating to deal with.

It is easy to be unhappy, weary, worn-out, uninterested, and irritated in life. Discouragement sets in when you allow yourself the perilous perk of self-pity. Thoughts come to you like:

"Nobody appreciates me."

"Even my own children won't listen to me."

"I'm really not achieving anything."

If you really understand your relationship to God, you will not spend any time questioning, "What have I done to deserve this?" or "What does God have against me?" Instead, you will shun self-pity and self-condemnation. "Don't judge, so that you won't be judged," has direct reference to you and your relationship with God. (Matthew 7:1).

A proper attitude is a priceless possession. Proper self-image will help keep you in pleasing pathways. Abraham Lincoln said, "It is difficult to make a man miserable while he feels he is worthy of himself and claims kindred to the great God who made him." (In The International Thesaurus of Quotations, comp. Rhoda Thomas Tripp, New York: Thomas Y. Crowell Co., 1970, p. 575.)

Proper self-image is a great asset. It is a virtue to understand who you are and to act accordingly. Being created in God's likeness is a wonderful blessing. He said, "Don't you know that you are a temple of God, and that God's Spirit lives in you? If anyone destroys the temple of God, God will destroy him; for God's temple is holy, which you are." (1 Corinthians 3:16-17). Proper self-image is necessary to be purposeful and effective in God's work.

Dr. Thomas Harris stated, "Most people never fulfill their human promise and potential because they remain perpetually helpless children overwhelmed by a sense of inferiority. The feeling of being okay does not imply that the person has risen above all his faults and emotional problems. It merely implies that he refuses to be paralyzed by them. He is determined to accept himself as he is but also to assume more and more control of his life."

You came to this earth for experience, and that is all you can take out of it. You decide for yourself what you will do with your life. The future belongs to those who know what to do with it. Look forward to the unknown with faith, optimism and confidence. Look to tomorrow with joyful expectation, realizing that with God's help you can do all things.

You need to constantly build faith in yourself. Faith makes it possible to know that in every failure or setback, there is always a next time, another chance to succeed. Children of God are living below their capabilities. Achieve, conquer, and overcome! Your efforts today will determine your location tomorrow.

Norman Vincent Peale advises to "believe in yourself! Have faith in your abilities! Without a humble but reasonable confidence in your own powers you cannot be successful or happy." The fears in your life can be conquered if you have faith and move forward with purpose. Fear inhibits progress but the roadblocks to progress are cast aside when you resolve never to walk alone. Recognize that with God's help, nothing is impossible for you.

Even if you feel you are behind in life's race, you are not losing if you are moving in the right direction. God will not score your performance until the end of the journey. He expects you to be victorious. He stands anxiously by to answer your call for help. Only you can determine what you do with what happens to you. And what you do with what happens to you is much more important than what happens to you. With God's help you can do what is right.

"Everything always works out for the best, in unexpected and miraculous ways. Don't waste time worrying about how things will be resolved— just keep the faith."

Chapter 5

Be Not Faithless

On the day of the resurrection Jesus appeared to ten of the twelve apostles. Thomas was not with them at the time. When the others told Thomas, "We have seen the Lord," he countered, "Unless I see in his hands the print of the nails, and put my finger into the print of the nails, and put my hand into his side, I will not believe."

Eight days later all eleven apostles were together. "Jesus came, the doors being locked, and stood in the midst, and said, Peace be to you."

To Thomas, He said, "Reach here your finger, and see my hands. And reach here your hand, and put it into my side. Don't be faithless, but believing."

An astounded Thomas answered, "My Lord and my God."

Then Jesus said to him, "Because you have seen me, you have believed. Blessed are those who have not seen, and have believed." (John 20:25-29).

I have met a lot of people who think like Thomas. They demand empirical evidence. They require confirmation before they will believe anything. That is the dialect of the world today. Doubting Thomas has become the moniker of those who refuse to accept anything they cannot physically prove and explain. Faith challenges our soul to travel beyond what our eyes perceive.

If you have doubts, hear the words spoken to Thomas as he touched Jesus' wounded hands: "Be not faithless, but believing." God has a perfect plan for each one of us. He doesn't reveal His plan all at once but offers us direction one step at a time because He wants us to learn to walk by faith and not by sight.

Everything always works out for the best, in unexpected and miraculous ways. Don't waste time worrying about how things will be resolved—just keep the faith. Fear and worry are dispelled through faith in the Lord Jesus Christ. Believe in Jesus Christ, the Son of God, and the greatest person of all time.

Believe that He is the Messiah of the New Testament, that He died on the cross and was resurrected, and that He lives, the Son of God, our Savior and our Redeemer!

It is always easy to quit and give up. It takes faith to keep going and move on through. The Apostle John affirmed "all things were made through [God]. Without him was not anything made that has been made." (John 1:3). And yet we stroll beneath the stars at night, feel the touch of spring on the earth and still doubt the hand of Divinity in creation. Do we forget or do we just deny the words of the Psalmist when he said, "The heavens declare the glory of God? The expanse shows his handiwork. Day after day they pour forth speech. And night after night they display knowledge. There is no speech nor language where their voice is not heard." (Psalm 19:1-3)? All the beauty of earth bears the fingerprint of God.

Believe that Isaiah anticipated the coming of a promised Messiah, asserting, "Therefore the Lord himself will give you a sign; behold, a virgin shall conceive, and bear a son, and shall call his name Immanuel." (Isaiah 7:14).

"And the government shall be on his shoulder: and his name shall be called Wonderful,

Counselor, Mighty God, Everlasting Father, Prince of Peace." (Isaiah 9:6).

Believe that He who was born in a manger when there was no room in the inn is the Son of God. Have faith that there was an angelic chorus that sang at His birth; that shepherds worshipped Him; that a new star appeared in the east; and that wise men traveled from far off bringing Him gold, frankincense, and myrrh.

Believe that John the Baptist declared, "Behold the Lamb of God, who takes away the sin of the world." (John 1:29). Trust the voice of the Almighty declaring above the waters of Jordan, "This is my beloved Son, in whom I am well pleased." (Matthew 3:17).

Believe that Christ was a man of miracles. At Cana He turned the water into wine. He caused the lame to walk, the blind to see, the dead to return to life. Know that this Master Physician healed the sick by His inherent power as the Son of God.

Believe that He comforted the troubled multitudes of His time. Today, He offers that same comfort to everyone who truthfully has faith in Him. "Come to me," He says to us, "all you who labor and are heavily burdened, and I will give you rest. Take my yoke on you, and learn from me; for I am humble and lowly in heart: and you will find rest for your souls. For my yoke is easy, and my burden is light." (Matthew 11:28-30).

Believe that Jesus is the Ruler of life and death. He proclaimed His everlasting power to the grief-stricken Martha, stating, "I am the resurrection, and the life. He who believes in me, though he die, yet will he live. Whoever lives and believes in me will never die." (John 11:25-26).

Thomas was there when Jesus expressed those words and also when Lazarus was subsequently summoned out of the sepulcher. Yet he doubted the Lord's power to raise Himself after His horrendous death on the cross, asserting to the other apostles that unless he could feel the wounds in His hands, he would not believe.

Like Thomas, we may also be inclined to overlook the signs of His perfect life and power. We should instead remember the admonition of Paul to the Ephesian saints when he wrote,

"Finally, be strong in the Lord, and in the strength of his might. Put on the whole armor of God, that you may be able to stand against the wiles of the devil....Stand therefore, having the utility belt of truth buckled around your waist, and having put on the breastplate of righteousness, and having fitted your feet with the preparation of the gospel of peace; above all, taking up the shield of faith, with which you will be able to quench all the fiery darts of the evil one." (Ephesians 6:10-11, 14-16). Remember that worry ends when faith in God begins.

While traveling through Samaria, Jesus became fatigued and thirsty. He paused at Jacob's well and begged for a drink from a woman who had come to draw water. In the discussion that ensued, He affirmed the saving power of His gospel, saying, "Everyone who drinks of this water will thirst again, but whoever drinks of the water that I will give him will never thirst; but the water that I will give him will become in him a well of water springing up to everlasting life." (John 4:13-14).

In that conversation the woman spoke of the promised Messiah, "he who is called Christ." Jesus unambiguously announced to her, "I who speak to you am he." (John 4:25-26).

Unquestionably, personal faith is the basis of the gospel and essential to us as individuals. This source of power and of action is vital to our salvation and of absolute importance to us. All Christians should take every opportunity to develop faith, both in their own lives and in the lives of others. As Christians, faith is our heritage.

Paul instructed us to be "an example to those who believe, in word, in your way of life, in love, in spirit, in faith, and in purity." (1 Timothy 4:12).

Faith is the power of God by which the universe was made. It is a gift from God to those who believe in Him. No living, knowledgeable person, whether serving God or not, acts without faith. You might as well try to live without breathing as to live without the principle of faith. But you must believe in the truth, obey the truth, and practice the truth, to attain the power of God called faith. Faith ultimately comes from within.

"No challenge in life, no obstacle in our path is too powerful that it cannot be overcome with faith."

Rich Nelson

Chapter 6

Faith – The Force of Life

Life can be difficult and challenging. At every stage of life there will be hardships to endure and problems to conquer. You may suffer the despair of feeling victimized or rejected. Growing up can be awkward. Seeking an education can push you to your financial limits. The struggles associated with marriage, starting a family and making a living can be arduous. Dealing with physical illness, old age, and death are the realities of life that we are required to meet.

But you can face and solve these challenges more freely and fearlessly when you understand that problems are a normal part of living. When we have faith in Jesus Christ, the most difficult challenges as well as our most pleasant circumstances can be a blessing. No challenge in life, no obstacle in our path is too powerful that it cannot be overcome with faith.

"The great thing," wrote C. S. Lewis, "is to stop regarding all the unpleasant things as interruptions of one's 'own,' or 'real' life. The truth is of course that what one calls the interruptions are precisely one's real life-the life God is sending one day by day". (They Stand Together: The Letters of C. S. Lewis to Arthur Greeves, ed. Walter Hooper, London: Collins, 1979, p. 499).

Maybe you feel that life is harsh and unfair. You may want to withdraw into your own little realm and never venture out into the real world denying you the chance to progress and live all the experiences that life might afford to you. But Jesus has made a power available to you that will turn your challenges into opportunities, a power that will enable you to appreciate Peter's statement that the trials of our faith are more valuable than gold. (See 1 Peter 1:7.)

The famous Russian writer Leo Tolstoy declared, "Faith is the force of life." Tolstoy learned that you can have almost everything you could possibly want of earthly gratification and glory; but without faith in God, life would simply be a burden to your heart, mind and soul.

Tolstoy spent most of his life trying to understand the purpose of life. He had fame, fortune, and social status. He married well and had a family. He experienced success by nearly every measure the world uses. He searched for answers to the meaning of life in his studies of science, philosophy, and other fields of knowledge. Still, all he had acquired, his knowledge, his honors, and his personal accomplishments, brought him no permanent satisfaction. Life still seemed meaningless.

At a personal point of deep despair, Tolstoy asked, "How am I to live?"

The answer he received was: "By the Law of God."

Tolstoy finally came to understand that "besides the reasoning knowledge, [there is] in every living man another kind of knowledge, an unreasoning one, but which gives a possibility of living-faith. Faith is the force of life." (How I Came to Believe, Christchurch, New Zealand: The Free Age Press, 1901, p. 40.)

Perhaps you feel that life would not be so hard if you had more money or a higher social station or if you were liked better by your peers. Maybe you feel that if you got married, then you could be truly happy. Or possibly you are wishing you were free from the responsibilities of marriage, thinking that your life would be easier. Maybe you believe that the problems others face are not quite as hard as your own.

Not every challenge consists of a physical or material nature. As different as all of our challenges may be, the strength to meet them comes from the same source: faith in God. Believing in God and seeking to live His law will provide you with the power to successfully overcome the challenges that life brings. It has been said that faith is not knowing what the future holds but knowing who holds the future.

Faith in God helps you foster a personal love for Him, one that is reciprocated by Him through blessing you in your greatest times of need. Do not dread the trials of time; approach them with faith in God. God will reward your faith with power to endure and to overcome adversities, frustrations, anxieties, and all the complexities of day-to-day living. With faith in God you will not turn away from His everlasting course, nor be dissuaded by the ways or the praise of the world.

If you are under a mountain of school work and unable to accomplish as much as you'd like, can faith move that mountain? Can faith move the mountain standing between you and your ideal career? Does a mountain of trouble surround you in your marriage or your family? Or are you faced with a mountain of bills you can't seem to get over? Can faith in the Lord Jesus Christ move these mountains from your life?

People constantly try to face difficult problems on their own. They often choose the worst and then hope for the best. They do not understand how to use their faith to make good things happen for them, to manifest miracles and move mountains and to righteously triumph over any situation.

The most straightforward description of faith that I have ever seen is "faith is power." But how do you harness that power and use your faith to resolve the challenges of life? How do you use faith to move the mountains in your life?

Here are six specific suggestions:

1. Believe.

Do you believe the things that Jesus taught? Are you able to exercise faith in God with little or no tangible evidence? Unbelief is the killer of faith. How much proof do you need before you act in faith? Faith is never built on physical substantiation. You must first exercise your faith, then miracles will follow. Spiritual evidence will come as you believe and commit.

2. Commit.

Decide what you want, commit to obtain it, and exercise your faith until you do. Keep spiritual priorities foremost in your mind and heart until you reach your righteous desire.

Faith in the Lord Jesus Christ is fully sustaining. You can cause things to happen by disciplining yourself and paying the price. Be truly committed, and you will see the mountains move in your behalf.

"All things are possible to him who believes". (Mark 9:23). Commit yourself in advance to what you want. Faith will bring it about if you act.

3. Act.

Don't expect the Lord to do more than His part. When you do everything in your power, then God will come and save you in your hour of need. As James taught us, "and by works faith was perfected". (James 2:22).

Pay the required price but also understand what type of payment God expects. The price most often required by the Lord is the sacrifice of your own personal sins. He wants you to give those up to Him.

Do everything in your power to do your part, then pray.

4. Pray.

Pray as if everything depended upon God. Ask Him for the gift of faith. Ask, and you shall receive.

Exercise great faith in your prayers. A loving and all-knowing God will provide you with everything you righteously desire. Pray and believe that you can move mountains, and they will, in the Lord's time, move; but you must also expect.

5. Expect.

Expect troubles. Misfortune builds faith. God will not tempt you, but He will test you. Problems and troubles are what make up this earthly life. Life is by nature an upstream battle. It is an uphill climb. Don't try to remove yourself from the current and don't sit waiting on the plateaus.

The struggles and complications you may be trying to avoid could be the very elements that sharpen you and make you better. The Lord will test every attribute you possess at every stage of your life and when He knows you are faithful, then anticipate.

6. Anticipate.

Expect the Lord to act according to your faith. He will move the mountains in your life. He will take care of you. God wants you to move mountains and He has promised you that you can. He wants you to use the power that resides in you to do good things in His way.

If you pray for something and it does not turn out the way you want it to, you must not lose faith. In the Lord's own way and time, all righteous prayers are answered, but His way and His time are not always the same as ours. When your prayers seem to go unanswered, it is because God is answering you in a larger way than you can even imagine.

Receive all that God gives you with a thankful heart. Job, after losing all he owned, said, "The Lord gave, and the Lord has taken away. Blessed be the name of the Lord". (Job 1:21).

If you are submissive, humble, and patient, the Lord will give you everything that is best for you.

God will hear and answer your prayers if you have faith in the Lord Jesus Christ. The Lord said, "For most assuredly I tell you, whoever may tell this mountain, 'Be taken up and cast into the sea', and doesn't doubt in his heart, but believes that what he says happens; he shall have whatever he says.

Therefore I tell you, all things whatever you pray and ask for, believe that you receive them, and you shall have them". (Mark 11:23-24).

Today is a day of miracles. Believe in miracles. Expect miracles according to your faith. Pray passionately. Actively seek to increase your faith, and with that great gift from God, you can cause great things to occur in your life.

Faith in Jesus Christ is fully sustaining. The Lord will move the mountains blocking your way in your schooling, in your employment, in your marriage, in your family. God is full of mercy, forgiveness, patience, and long-suffering. And Jesus will unlock the treasure house of blessings to anyone who is full of faith. Remember that Jesus is the key to heaven, but it is faith that unlocks the door.

Faith is power. It is a mystical, divine power that surpasses all we can possibly envision. It is the power by which God functions. It is a power that, over time, can also be yours if you desire it and seek it.

My faith is my guiding light and my foothold. It is conveyed by the Spirit and enhanced by prayer. It elevates my soul. It opens my heart. It nourishes my knowledge that God lives, and that Jesus is the

Christ. May the Lord bless us with the faith and the power to go forward in our lives.

5-star reviews are a blessing to Christian authors. If you found this book inspirational, educational or simply enjoyable, please post an honest review.

About the Author

Rich Nelson is the author of a variety of published articles on topics such as religious education, family values, health, and politics. His work has appeared in Christian Education Today, Church Teacher, Parish Teacher, Living with Teenagers, Liberty Magazine, and many others.

Contact Information:
Broken Hill Publications
Glenwood Springs, CO 91601

Email Rich at: rich@srnelson.com

Visit Rich at: www.srnelson.com

Other Books by Rich Nelson

Gaining Power through Prayer

Book 2 in The Powerful Christian Series

Sincere prayer is a fountain of divine power flowing into our lives. Through prayer we gain clear and precise direction. Through prayer we access the strength of character to perform God's will – to do what is right. Prayer is the process we use to place ourselves in contact with God.

The impressive power of prayer warrants the consideration not only of Christians, but of all societies. This little booklet highlights the principle applications and purposes of prayer. It confirms that God does answer our prayers and demonstrates how we can be more aware of those divine answers. It also examines the challenging question of why, at times, it appears that God does not answer us and what we can do about it.

The Added Power of Obedience

Book 3 in The Powerful Christian Series

Two opposing powers grapple in every human heart and our decisions are usually influenced by them, either to do good or to do evil. The spirit of truth will always persuade us to obey God. We all want happiness. We hope for it, live for it, and make it our primary goal in life. But do we live in a way that allows us to enjoy the happiness we desire so deeply?

The way to be happy is simply to believe in Jesus Christ and obey the gospel. When we obey God's law, then we can expect to find the happiness we desire. Obedience to God is not an inconvenience, it is our ultimate aspiration; it is not a stumbling block, it is a powerful and profitable building block.

The Healing Power of Forgiveness

Book 4 in The Powerful Christian Series

Repentance and forgiveness are the essence of the gospel of Jesus Christ. It is a principle that offers hope, expectation and encouragement to every believer.

The power of forgiveness brings great joy and peace to us. This infinite miracle is a direct result of the great mediation and atonement of Jesus Christ. This reconciliation, where Jesus through His own choice paid the price of our sins and mistakes, sanctifies and purifies us. It is indeed the greatest miracle of all miracles.

Faith in Jesus Christ teaches us that it is worth everything to continually cleanse and purify our lives through repentance. It is because of our faith in Him that we have the power to receive His forgiveness. The great blessing and miracle is that you and I have the very same power given to us. It is this inner power of forgiveness that changes lives. We are most like Jesus Christ when we forgive another person.

This is Life Eternal

Developing a Personal Relationship with Christ.

This is Life Eternal is a life changing book for any Christian who wishes to deepen his or her relationship with Jesus Christ. On many occasions Jesus has invited us to "know the truth". "Learn of me" Jesus says, "and you will find rest for your souls." (Matt. 11:29). Knowing Christ will change our lives. He is available to us, to guide and direct us and to give us a sense of purpose and a marvelous dimension to life. Coming to know Jesus can be a stimulating, rewarding, soul-transforming experience. It can ultimately make us free.

"Nelson's 'This is Life Eternal' is a step-by-step how-to book dealing with the most important relationship in life, the one between you and your Lord. Every Christian who is serious about a life devoted to God will find a powerful reawakening of spiritual desires. Nelson's book helped me break through the chaff of life and focus on the pure heart of what really matters, to develop a real and personal relationship with Christ. Every sincere Christian should read this book."

Excerpt from

Gaining Power Through Prayer

The Powerful Christian Series
Book 2

by S. Richard Nelson

available at www.srnelson.com

Excerpt:
Gaining Power through
Prayer

The greatest miracle of all communication is undeniably the awesome power of prayer! It never loses service or drops a call. It never breaks down. It has no "dead zones". We can never go over our minutes. It never limits the number of requests we may offer up in each prayer. It never goes to voicemail. Nothing can disconnect us from direct contact with God. He is reachable at any time and in any place.

God grants us the gratification of conversing directly with Him. He sets no restrictions as to time, place, or substance of our prayers. The Apostle Paul wrote, "In everything by prayer and petition with thanksgiving, let your requests be made known unto God." (Phil. 4:6 Italics added).

Each of us, at times, needs a little help in some aspect of our lives. Perhaps we are facing problems in our families. Maybe we are dealing with work or career issues. We could be undergoing financial difficulties or maybe we are struggling with personal shortcomings and imperfections.

The fundamental secret to success in any of these areas is prayer. Prayer is the source of spiritual power. When we discover how to obtain answers to prayer, we can tap into God's infinite power and goodness to assist us in our troubles. Without the power of prayer, we typically face our problems on our own.

Sincere believers shouldn't need to be encouraged to pray, and yet many do not say formal prayers. They do not consider what it means to their lives when they disregard the gift of prayer. When we fail to pray, we forfeit the promises that prayer tenders. Our lives should be infused with the influence of prayer and gratitude to God. We should never deny ourselves His power by disregarding the power of prayer.

Prayer lifts our thoughts to a higher and nobler plain; and leads our lives to worthier pursuits. It provides passage for the grace and glory of God to pass through and will illuminate, expand, elevate, and bless all those who avail themselves of its power.

Prayer's resolute power to transform our souls is unquestionable....

...Jesus said: "Behold, I stand at the door and knock. If anyone hears my voice and opens the door, I will come in to him, and will dine with him, and he with me." (Rev. 3:20)

This is a promise made to each one of us! There is no bias or favoritism. He stands and knocks. If we listen, we will hear His voice. If we open the door, He will come in and dine with us. He will answer our prayers. The Lord stands knocking. He never moves away. But we must open the door. He will never force Himself upon us. He won't break down the door. We are responsible for learning how to listen; how to find an answer; how to interpret and understand.

Within God's word we can easily find a promise that fits our need, whatever that need is. We can then go to God and say, "Lord, this is Your word; prove it's so by implementing it in my life. I believe in Your word; now make it happen according to my faith." We can expect a complete fulfillment of every sentence that God has spoken. Oblige the Lord with His own words, and expect Him to do as He has said, simply because He said it.

The promise of Revelation 3:20 is a summons to pray. It is the very substance of prayer. It says that we can approach God and say to Him, "This is Your word, Lord, now do what You said; please fulfill Your promise." This is, in essence, the power of prayer....

...Some seem to believe in prayer, but not in the power of prayer. They pray but do not actually expect God to answer them. We must have complete faith in the power of prayer. The prophet Hosea assures us that "The ways of the Lord are right." (Hosea 14:9). God will respond when we make honest petitions and open our hearts to His counsel and guidance.

Since God knows our hearts, when we are alone with Him, we can pray with increased intensity and feeling. We can drop any façade and charade. We can put aside our duplicity and our pride. We can abandon all insincerity and illusory deceit. Jesus went into the mountains alone to pray. Paul found his solitude in Arabia. He started out a worldly man and returned renewed, regenerated and reborn.

Have you ever prayed with similar intensity? Have you ever prayed for an entire day? Have you prayed for an hour or even half an hour? Or do you pray for just ten minutes out of every twenty-four hours?

Our prayers can usually be counted in seconds and yet, with such a paltry effort, we still expect God to answer us with abundance. God asks us to pray "evening, morning, and at noon" (Ps. 55:17), and to "pray without ceasing." (1 Thes. 5:17). We cannot invest pennies in our prayers and expect thousands of dollars in return.

Sometimes we lack the faith that God will hear and answer our prayers. Perhaps we haven't recently recognized a response when we pray. Consequently, our attempts to pray, if we pray at all, become shallow and superficial. We pray, but don't persevere long enough or patiently enough for a reply. We can feel, therefore, that our prayers go unanswered.

Jesus' advice to us regarding the great second coming was to watch, "for you do not know in what hour your Lord comes." (Matt. 24:42). This same advice applies also to the peaceful, quiet moments He comes silently and secretly in answer to our heartfelt supplications....

...All of us can learn by observation and study and by reading the philosophies and ideologies shared in books. We gain a greater value, however, from the learning that comes directly from God. It will enlighten our thoughts and enrich our emotions.

The messages and teachings from God will have a profound transformational effect on our lives.

This transformation is available to all of us if we humbly and earnestly pursue it. If we ask, God will award us the blessings He wishes to impart. He will give us encouragement, motivation and divine direction in every aspect of our lives.

The purpose of prayer, ultimately, is to give us a new birth and to draw us closer to God.

Read more *Gaining Power through Prayer* at:

www.srnelson.com

www.ingramcontent.com/pod-product-compliance
Lightning Source LLC
Chambersburg PA
CBHW060650030426
42337CB00017B/2538